Guide of
ROME
Kids

Archeolibri

ArcheoJunior

All about Rome

Country: Italy. **Region:** Lazio
Size: 1,287.36 square kilometers or 497 square miles
Population: 2,848,000
Residents: Romans
Patron Saints: Saint Peter and Saint Paul

Feast Day: June 29th
Nicknames: Eternal City, *Urbe*, *Caput Mundi*
Motto: *Senatus Populusque Romanus* (the Roman Senate and People, often abbreviated as SPQR)

Ancient History of Rome

This splendid city, the capital of Italy, is rich in history and art. It truly lives up to its Latin nickname **caput mundi**, which means "capital of the world." Rome was once the center of an enormous empire that included not only the areas we know today as Italy and Europe, but also North Africa and the Middle East. Since 313 A.D. it has gained even more importance, becoming the center of Christianity and home to the popes and eventually the capital of Italy. Traces of this ancient empire can still be seen all over Rome, a fascinating place where history comes to life!

THE MYTH OF THE WOLF OF ROME

According to legend, in ancient Latium there were two brothers, Amulius and Numitor, who were battling to take control of the city of Alba Longa. Amulius managed to oust his brother and then forced Numitor's daughter, Rhea Silvia, to become a vestal virgin, a kind of priestess in the temple who could never marry or have children. That ensured that she would not have any heirs who might challenge his claim to the throne. But young Rhea Silvia was seduced by the god Mars and gave birth to twins named **Romulus and Remus**. Her uncle was furious and ordered the infants to be killed immediately. The guard who was supposed to do the deed could not bring himself to kill them, though, so he hid the babies in a basket and set it afloat on the Tiber, hoping that someone would find them and take care of them. Luckily, a she-wolf had gone down to the river to get a drink near the Palatine Hill. She heard the infants crying and brought them onto the riverbank, where she warmed them up and nursed them with her own milk. Then Romulus, the legend continues, went on to found the city of Rome!

Before the foundation of Rome, the small hills around the river Tiber were only scattered with small villages, because often the valleys were swampy and less easy to defend. Over time, the villages united through wars or alliances, and this is how Rome was born!
The seven hills were the uplands on which Rome was first built, evidence of which can still be seen in the old city centre today. They were approximately 50 meters high, but were modified over the centuries as the city expanded. As documented by ancient Latin authors, the hills were called: **Aventino, Campidoglio, Celio, Esquilino, Palatino, Quirinale, Viminale** (Aventine, Capitoline, Celian, Esquiline, Palatine, Quirinal, Viminal).

ROME OVER THE CENTURIES

10th-9th cent. BC

Bronze and Iron Age

Villages in the Lazio region.

Foundation of Rome (753 BC).

8th-6th cent. BC

Royal Period

Rome conquered Alba Longa (641 BC).

Roman–Etruscan Wars (6th-5th centuries BC).

5th cent. BC

Rome expelled Tarquinius Superbus and the Republic was born (509 BC).

Wars against the Italic, Volsci, Aequi, Hernici, Sabine and Latin peoples (5th century BC).

4th cent. BC

Rome destroyed the Etruscan city of Veii (395 BC).
Rome invaded by the Gauls (390 BC).
Conflict between the Patrician and Plebeian classes.
First written laws (4th century BC).

First Samnite War (343-341 BC).
Latin War ending in the dissolution of the Latin League (340-338 BC).
Second Samnite War (326-304 BC).
Third Samnite War (298-290 BC).

3rd cent. BC

Republican Period

First Punic War (264-241 BC), Sicily became a Roman province. The Romans occupied Sardinia, Sicily and Corsica (237 BC).

2nd cent. BC

Second Punic War (218-201 BC). During the 2nd century BC, the Romans conquered most of the territories bordering the Mediterranean, creating new provinces such as Greece, Asia, Africa and Gaul. Third Punic War (149-146 BC).

GAIUS IULIUS CAESAR

1st cent. BC

Social War, Rome granted citizenship to the Italic peoples (91-89 BC).
Feud between Marius and Sulla (88-86 BC), Sulla's dictatorship (82-79 BC).
First Triumvirate: Caesar, Pompey and Crassus (60-53 BC), civil war between Caesar and Pompey (49-45 BC), Death of Caesar (44 BC).
Second Triumvirate: Octavian, Anthony and Lepidus.
Octavian defeated Anthony and Cleopatra in the battle of Actium (31 BC).

Octavian (Augustus) became the first emperor (27 BC-14 AD).
Architecture, arts and literature flourished.
Birth of Jesus Christ in Palestine (year zero).

Nero (54-68), the Domus Aurea was built. The Great Fire of Rome (64).
Vespasian (69-79), first Jewish-Roman War and the conquest of Jerusalem (70).
Eruption of Mount Vesuvius and the destruction of Pompeii,
Herculaneum and Stabia (79).
Titus (79-81). Inauguration of the Colosseum (80).

Trajan (98-117), conquest of Dacia, Trajan's forum, markets and column
were built. Maximum expansion of the Empire.
Hadrian (117-138), construction of Hadrian's Wall in Britain and
Hadrian's Villa in Tivoli, reconstruction of the Pantheon in Rome.

Imperial Period

Marcus Aurelius (161-180), Parthian War (161/2-166), trade with the
Chinese Empire, Marcomannic Wars in Germany, the Antonine Plague
(perhaps a measles epidemic).
Commodus (180-192), the end of persecution against Christians.
Septimius Severus (193-211), wars against the Parthians (197-199)
and construction of the triumphal arch.
Caracalla (211-217), Roman citizenship to all free citizens in the Empire,
construction of the largest thermal baths in Rome.

Aurelian (270-275), barbarian invasions curbed, construction of new
walls around Rome.
Diocletian (284-305), end of military anarchy, severe persecution of
Christians.

Imperial Period

Middle Ages

Renaissance

Maxentius (306-312), extensive construction works, including the Temple of Romulus, the Basilica of Maxentius, the Villa and Circus of Maxentius, to name but a few.
Constantine (306-337), Constantinople appointed the new capital of the Empire (330), freedom of worship for Christians (313).
Sack of Rome, carried out by the Visigoths (410).

Romulus Augustus, the last emperor, deposed by Odoacer, marking the end of the Western Roman Empire (476).

The Ostrogothic Kingdom of Italy was established (493).
The Lombards invaded Italy and took many territories from the Eastern Empire in northern Italy (568).

On Christmas Day, in Rome, Pope Leo III crowned Charlemagne Emperor of the Holy Roman Empire (800).
Beginning of the power struggle between Pope Gregory VII and Emperor Henry IV (The Investiture Controversy, 1073-1085).
Rome semi-destroyed by the Normans, led by Robert Guiscard (1084).

Boniface VIII proclaimed the first Jubilee (1300).
Clement V transported the Papal See from Rome to Avignon (1305, where it remained until 1377).
Roman Republic established by Cola di Rienzo (1337-1354).

The Capitoline Museums were founded, and housed the oldest public collection in the world (1471).
Julius II began demolishing the old St. Peter's Basilica, later building the current basilica under the supervision of the architect Bramante (1503-1513).
Michelangelo painted the frescoes in the Sistine Chapel (1508-1541).
Leo X, son of Lorenzo the Magnificent, made Rome the center of Renaissance culture (1513-1521). The Lutheran Reformation began under his pontificate. The ensuing struggles were followed by the ruinous Sack of Rome by the imperial troops of Charles V of Habsburg (1527).
Jacobin Republic in Rome; Pope Pius VI deported to France (1799).
The Restoration, Pope Pius VII returned to Rome (1814).

Roman Republic headed by the triumvirate Mazzini, Armellini, Saffi (1849). Giuseppe Garibaldi was the commander-in-chief of the Roman Republic Army. However, the French troops put an end to the Republican government, putting Pius IX back on the papal throne.

On September 20th, Italian troops entered Rome in the famous breach of Porta Pia. Rome was annexed to the Kingdom of Italy (1870).

First World War (1915-1918).
On February 11th, the Lateran Pacts resolved the so-called "Roman issue" between the Church and the Kingdom of Italy (1929).

Second World War (1939-1945).
The Nazi occupation of Rome (1943-1944).
In June 1944, Rome was liberated by Allied troops.
Italy was declared a Republic on June 2nd, 1946 following a popular referendum.

Rome experienced rapid population growth and new districts were built (1950-1980).

THE COLOSSEUM

Rome's most famous sight and the one most popular with tourists is the Colosseum, a symbol of the ancient Roman Empire. It's the largest amphitheater in the world.

It was built during the reign of Emperor Vespasian (69-79 AD), who wanted to give his people an entertainment building, and was inaugurated by his son Titus in 80 AD. As these emperors belonged to the gens Flavia, the Colosseum was also known as the "**Flavian Amphitheatre**".The Colosseum's size was staggering for its time. The outside wall was 50 meters (164 feet) high, and it was 156 meters (512 feet) wide and 188 meters (617 feet) long. More than 50,000 spectators could fit inside. In the central area, the cavea, was the arena, a wooden platform covered in sand where performances were staged.
Performances included gladiator fights and fights with fierce animals.
Before the underground tunnels were built, they also organised naval battles (*naumachiae*) inside the Colosseum, which was filled with water!

THE GLADIATORS

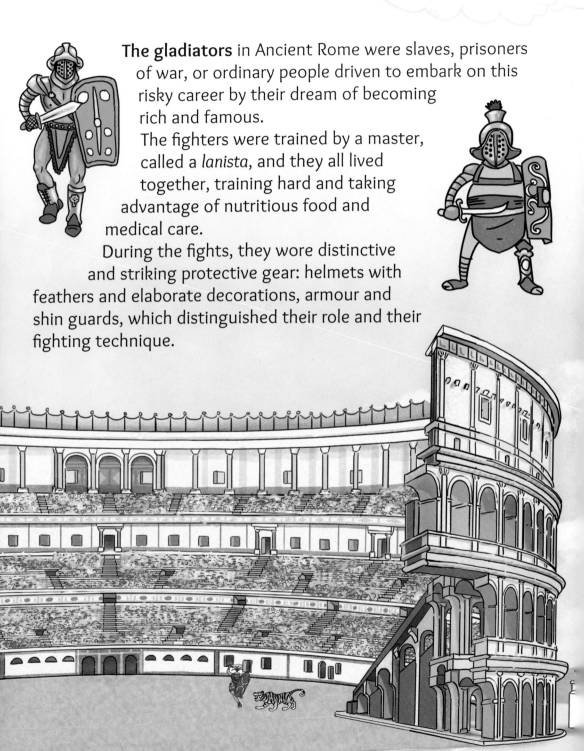

The gladiators in Ancient Rome were slaves, prisoners of war, or ordinary people driven to embark on this risky career by their dream of becoming rich and famous.

The fighters were trained by a master, called a *lanista*, and they all lived together, training hard and taking advantage of nutritious food and medical care.

During the fights, they wore distinctive and striking protective gear: helmets with feathers and elaborate decorations, armour and shin guards, which distinguished their role and their fighting technique.

THE COLOSSEUM VALLEY

The **Arch of Constantine** stands next to the Colosseum. It's over 20 metres high, making it the city's largest triumphal arch, through which the processions celebrating the return of a victorious general and his army entered the city. It was built in 315 to honour Emperor Constantine, who had beaten his rival Maxentius in 312.

It was built very quickly, using many elements from previous eras — for example reliefs, statues and friezes -- reusing a precious and by then rare material such as marble. Not many people know that you can also access it through a narrow spiral staircase, next to which there is the signature of Michelangelo, which he left during a visit!

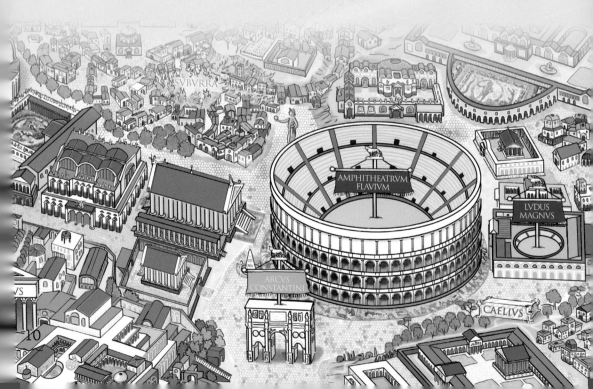

The **Domus Aurea**, Emperor Nero's grand and luxurious villa, once stood in the place of the Colosseum. The large Domus was surrounded by a huge park that extended from the Palatine Hill to the Esquiline Hill, and was filled with works of art and elegant decorations. After Nero died, all traces of him were erased and over time the villa was buried, only to be rediscovered, much to people's amazement, during the Renaissance.

Today, it can be visited from the park on the Oppian Hill. You can still see the incredible remains underground and the famous Octagon Room, once equipped with a mechanism to make it rotate!

Not far from the square in front of the Colosseum, there are also the remains of the **Ludus Magnus**, the largest and most prestigious gladiator training school in Rome, built by Emperor Domitian in the 1st century AD.

THE ROMAN FORUM

When we look at the remains of the **Roman Forum**, it's difficult to imagine what these places were like at the time of Romulus and Remus. The shepherds who lived on the uplands took their flocks down into the valley to drink, and they would meet up here to exchange livestock and goods. In the Republican Era, this area became the center of the city, a place where Roman citizens would meet to discuss politics, economics and anything else concerning public life.

The **Via Sacra**, which led to the Capitoline Hill, went through the Roman Forum, and was used by the processions celebrating victorious generals. Over the road, there is the **Arch of Titus**, built by the Senate after the emperor's death, in remembrance of his conquest of Jerusalem in 70 AD.

THE IMPERIAL FORUMS

The **Imperial Forums** are made up of a series of grand buildings and squares, which were built between the Late Republic and the Middle Empire to celebrate the grandeur of Rome. It includes the Forums of Caesar, Augustus, Nerva and Trajan.

Today, the Roman Forum and Imperial Forums are a vast archaeological site that is well-worth a visit. It's divided by **Via dei Fori Imperiali**, a long, straight road that was built in the 1930s.

A view of the Roman Forum with the Temple of Saturn, the Temple of Vespasian and the Temple of Concord.

THE TRAJAN'S FORUM AND MARKETS

Emperor Trajan had a huge forum built on the Quirinal Hill to commemorate his victories in Eastern Europe. The majestic **Trajan's Column** was in the large square where political and social gatherings took place. The monument is decorated with a spiralling frieze that winds around the column, depicting the wars in Dacia. The emperor's ashes were buried at the base.

The two **Library** buildings — one Greek, one Latin — were on either side of the column, and they housed thousands of precious books on antiquity.

Below the forum, on the side of the hill, there were the buildings of the monumental **Trajan Markets**, where the Romans could trade and buy all kinds of goods from across the empire.

They consisted of a semi-circular three-storey building, with a wonderful view of the forum and shops covered by a portico, and a second larger building that housed a grand hall with a vaulted ceiling, used as venue for large public events.

THE PALATIN HILL

According to legend, the **Palatine Hill** is where Romulus founded Rome. It was home to the kings during the Regal Period, and was where rich patrician families built their residences in the Republican Age.

In the Imperial Period, it was where the emperor's chose to live: the palaces of Augustus, Tiberius, Caligula, the Flavians and Septimius Severus were all built here, along with temples and the **Palatine Stadium** (image below).

THE CIRCUS MAXIMUS

The Circus Maximus was a stadium for chariot races — a very popular sport in ancient Rome! Inside the stadium there was a track and there were seats for 250,000 people! Today, the large space is used as a venue for public events, for jogging, or just as somewhere to stop and admire the ancient ruins.

The Romans staged races with carriages called **chariots**. They were often pulled by one or more horses, but sometimes ostriches or camels pulled the chariots! The winner of a race was rewarded with money, a wreath of laurels and palm fronds!

THE BATHS OF CARACALLA

The thermal baths built under the reign of Emperor **Caracalla**, were part of a grandiose public complex that was open to all Romans. It covered an area of 12,000 square meters and was made up of majestic buildings, cold and heated pools, gyms, saunas and rooms for events.

BATH TIME

The baths were the ideal place to wash, relax, chat, meet friends and conclude business.
There were three separate entrances: one for men, one for women and a third for slaves. Children weren't allowed inside.

THE AQUEDUCTS

Today, Rome uses **11 ancient aqueducts** and 5 modern ones for its water supply, but between 312 BC (when the water from the Tiber was no longer sufficient) and 537 AD (when they were cut off by the barbarian Ostrogoths), the ancient aqueducts were a marvel of engineering. They crossed large valleys and cut through hills, supplying the city with over one million cubic meters of water a day, which was used to supply a few privileged private houses, numerous public and monumental fountains, all the pools and public baths, and artificial lakes for naval battles.

The building technique was complex and well organised, skilfully taking advantage of sloping land and a network of dams. There was a duct, often mostly underground, and one or more sedimentation tanks which allowed impurities to settle on the bottom. The ducts that crossed basins were supported by arches that could also serve as bridges over roads.

THE FORUM BOARIUM AND THE GHETTO

Since ancient times, the **Forum Boarium** — which was where the square with the Mouth of Truth is today — was a place where livestock was traded and home to the market on the banks of the Tiber, extremely important for religious and commercial activities. Behind it is the **Porticus of Octavia**, a large arch built in honour of Emperor Augustus' sister. Nearby, there is the Roman quarter of the **Ghetto**, where the Roman Jews were segregated between the sixteenth and nineteenth centuries. Today, it is home to a large synagogue, built in 1904, which is still attended by many Hebrews.

BOCCA DELLA VERITÀ

The **Bocca della Verità** (Italian for "mouth of truth") is a large man's face carved in stone with a beard and eyes and an open mouth. Believe it or not, it was originally a manhole cover! It represented a river god swallowing the rainwater from the streets and taking it to the Tiber through Rome's largest sewer, the **Cloaca Maxima**. Today, it is in the portico of the ancient church of **Saint Mary in Cosmedin** (image above). A legend that dates back to the Middle Ages says that if you place your hand in the mouth and tell a lie, it will bite your hand!

THE AVENTINE HILL

In the Imperial Period, **Aventine Hill** was a wealthy residential area. In the Christian era, prestigious churches were built, such as the ancient **Saint Sabina**, with its original 5th-century wooden portal, and **Saint Alexis**, with its Romanesque-style bell tower and crypt. In the door to the garden of the Priory of the Knights of Malta, there's a curious secret: if you look through the key hole, you can see the **Dome of St. Peter's**!

This peaceful green hill is also home to **Rome's Rose Garden** (image below) and **Orange Tree Garden**, from where you can enjoy an incredible view of the city.

Piazza Navona

This area was originally a stadium for athletics competitions, commissioned by Emperor Domitian. It was very large and could hold 30,000 spectators. The ruins of the ancient **Stadium of Domitian** can be visited in the Underground Tunnels of Piazza Navona, but on the surface, you can still get an idea of its elongated shape, suitable for running races. The stands for the spectators were where the buildings surrounding the square are today. The original name of the square, in fact, came from the Latin *in agonis* (games).

In the Baroque period, Bernini built his famous **Fountain of the Four Rivers**, and the beautiful **Church of St. Agnes in Agone** was designed by his rival Borromini. Up until the 19th century, this square was flooded every summer and transformed into a water park for the Romans!

Campo de' Fiori

Campo de' Fiori was where public executions once took place. On February 17th, 1600, the philosopher **Giordano Bruno** was burned at the stake for heresy, as commemorated by Ferrari's statue in the center of the square, erected in 1887.
Today, a traditional lively **market** is held here every morning.

THE PANTHEON

The **Pantheon** is an emblem of Rome and one of its most famous monuments, but it has a Greek name. Pantheon means "temple of all the gods." It was originally built in the 1st century BC by **Agrippa**, Emperor Augustus' son-in-law, and later rebuilt under Hadrian after a terrible fire.

It became a Catholic church in 609, making it possible to preserve it to this day, and many important figures of the past are buried there.

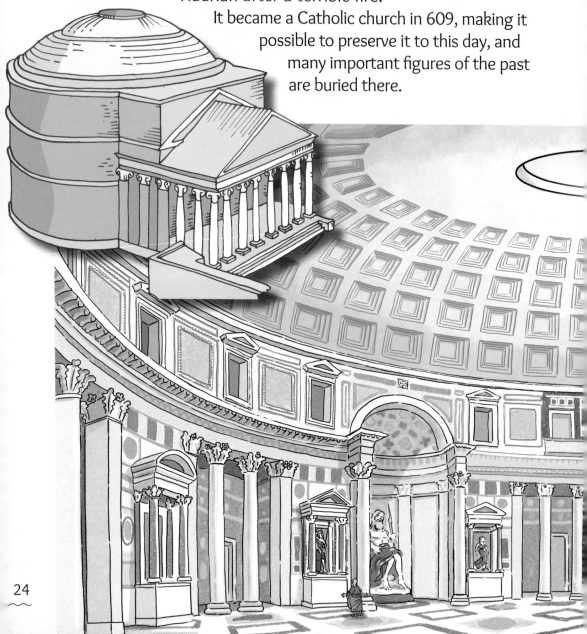

The building consists of a *pronaos* with eight columns, a rectangular structure and a large round room. The dome on top of this temple is unique, due in part to the presence of a small window called an *oculus* that allows light to enter. Rain also enters through that *oculus*, so there are 22 holes in the floor that allow the water to drain out. Legend has it that even when it rains, the Pantheon never gets wet. There's a reason for that impression: since hot air rises, it moves up toward the opening and causes much of the rainwater to evaporate. Any water that does reach the floor of the Pantheon goes down the drains!

Raffaello Sanzio, the famous painter of the Sistine Madonna, is also buried inside the Pantheon! Even if you don't recognize the name of the painting, you've probably seen it — especially the two little winged cherubs resting their chins in their hands as big fluffy clouds float behind them.

THE TREVI FOUNTAIN

This magnificent travertine and Carrara marble monument is one of the most famous fountains in the world!

The fountain sits in front of the **Palazzo Poli**. To reach it you have to walk down several narrow streets. That makes it even more dramatic when you step into the square and first glimpse the fountain — you feel as if you were traveling down a river into the wide open sea.

Architect Nicola Salvi combined classical and baroque motifs to design the 18th-century fountain. It depicts Neptune, the Roman god of the sea, with shells and tritons, and the niches on the sides house statues that represent health and abundance.

The Trevi Fountain is a Roman landmark and has been the subject of many legends and superstitions over the years. It has also been painted and drawn by many artists. One widely circulated story about the fountain says that if you turn your back to it and throw a **coin** over your shoulder into the water, you will be guaranteed to return to Rome. Hopeful tourists toss coins into the fountain all day long. The city of Rome collects the money and donates it to charity. The fountain "earns" about 3,000 euros a day!

ROME'S FOUNTAINS

Rome has always had a special relationship with water, as evidenced by the presence of around **2000 fountains**!
There were numerous natural springs in Rome when it was first built, which over time were used to create public fountains, thanks to a complex water system and the construction of aqueducts. From the Renaissance onwards, the Popes and important politicians wanted to enrich the city with fountains that reflected their wealth, and during the Baroque period the city's most beautiful and largest monumental fountains were built. Rome also has many smaller and more particular fountains, each with its own beautiful story to tell...

NASONI
All around the city there are small water fountains (about 2,500 of them) called *nasoni*, or big noses, because their faucets look like noses!

Piazza Venezia

This famous square takes its name from **Palazzo Venezia**, the large Renaissance building that Pope Paul II, still a cardinal at the time, had built in 1455 to demonstrate his generosity. The white marble monument, known as **Vittoriano** (image below), is dedicated to Vittorio Emanuele II, the first king of Italy, and it stands at the foot of the Capitoline Hill, where the city's medieval districts once were.

The monument is crowned by two huge quadrigae, built in 1908, each with a statue of a winged Victory, and they are one of the city's most famous landmarks.

In the center, there is the **Altar of the Fatherland**, with the Tomb of the Unknown Soldier, a memorial to the fallen soldiers in the First World War.

The hill behind it is the **Capitoline**, one of the seven hills on which Rome was founded. Today, the building is the headquarters of the Municipality of Rome and also houses the **Capitoline Museums**, in front of which there is the large bronze Equestrian Statue of Marcus Aurelius.

Piazza del Popolo

It's a very large square with a symmetrical shape, built at the beginning of the nineteenth century by the famous architect Valadier. The **Flaminio obelisk** stands in the center, brought to Rome by Emperor Augustus and placed here by the architect Fontana in 1589.

On the north side of the square, there's the **Church of Santa Maria del Popolo**, which contains many important works of art, including paintings by Pinturicchio, Caravaggio and Raphael.

ALONG VIA DEL CORSO

Via del Corso is a long, straight road that crosses the city center from Piazza del Popolo to Piazza Venezia, overlooked by important churches and sumptuous buildings. Running off it, there are beautiful streets with the most elegant Italian clothes shops, such as Via Condotti, Via del Babuino, Via Margutta and Via Frattina.

Along Via del Corso you can find — among other things — **Palazzo Doria Pamphilj**, which houses a Gallery with important Renaissance and Baroque paintings, the distinctive **Church of St. Ignatius** and, in the lovely little Piazza di Pietra, the ancient ruins of **Hadrian's temple.** Halfway along, there's Piazza Colonna, home to the Column of Marcus Aurelius, which is overlooked by **Palazzo Chigi**, seat of the Presidency of the Council of Ministers, and **Palazzo di Montecitorio**, seat of the Chamber of Deputies.

PIAZZA DI SPAGNA

Piazza di Spagna, home to the **Spanish Steps**, is one of the most famous places in the world.

In the center of the square there is a curious fountain in the shape of a boat, the **Barcaccia**, made by Pietro Bernini, father of the famous Gian Lorenzo. The boat is half sunk and overflowing with water. The sculptor probably got his inspiration from a boat left in the square after the river Tiber flooded!

Going up the beautiful Spanish Steps, built in 1725, you can enjoy a magnificent view.

There are 136 steps, but the ramps are so beautiful that you don't even notice the fatigue!

The Renaissance Church of **Trinità dei Monti** (image above) has two domes, and there's an ancient Egyptian obelisk in front of its facade.

VATICAN CITY

There is a small separate country located in Rome: **Vatican City**. Vatican City is the property of the Catholic Church, and it's the smallest country in the world with a population of just 900. One of those 900 people is the **pope**! The Vatican City coat of arms has two keys on it.
The gold key symbolizes heaven, while the silver key represents the pope.

WHITE SMOKE OR BLACK SMOKE?

When the pope dies, the College of Cardinals meets to elect the next pope. These meetings, known as **conclaves**, last for many days. They are top secret and very private.
The College of Cardinals communicates with the outside world using smoke. White smoke indicates that a new pope has been elected, but black smoke means that no new pope has been chosen yet.

THE SAINT PETER'S BASILICA

This huge Catholic Basilica, built over the **Tomb of the Apostle Peter**, is the symbol of the Vatican State. It's 130 meters high and covers an area of 22,000 square meters.

It was built in the Constantinian era and then rebuilt and modified over the centuries to arrive at today's St Peter's, with Michelangelo's huge dome and the Latin cross plan designed by the architect Maderno in the 17th century. The Basilica contains many works of art, such as Michelangelo's **The Pity** and **The Chair of Saint Peter** by Bernini. St. Peter's Square, with Bernini's famous colonnade, is directly in front of the Basilica, and is at the end of the long Via della Conciliazione.

The harmonious structure of the oval-shaped colonnade is reminiscent of two embracing arms. There is an ancient Egyptian obelisk in the center of the square.

WHO CAN BE A SWISS GUARD?

You need to be Swiss, Catholic, at least 174 centimeters (5 feet 8 1/2 inches) tall and between 19 and 30 years of age!

The **Swiss Guards** wear a special uniform that is bright blue, red and yellow.

They also wear white gloves and white collars. Renaissance artists from the time of Raphael and Michelangelo designed these outfits!

THE VATICAN MUSEUMS

The **Vatican Museums** is one of the largest and most visited museum complexes in the world, housing the artistic wonders collected by popes over the centuries. They are made up of buildings, galleries and courtyards, inside which there's an **Egyptian section** and important collections of **Greek and Roman** masterpieces, with grandiose statues such as the *Laocoon*, the *Augustus of Prima Porta* and the *Belvedere Torso*, to name but a few.

The Vatican Museums also include the papal apartments frescoed by **Raphael** with the famous *School of Athens*, which portrays the greatest philosophers of antiquity.

THE SISTINE CHAPEL

The **Sistine Chapel** is important for both its art and its history. This is the spot where conclaves assemble to hold their secret meetings to elect the pope; it's also the site of other official ceremonies. The walls and ceiling are decorated with famous frescoes by **Michelangelo** that depict biblical scenes from the Old Testament and the New Testament.

The Sistine Chapel is very interesting. Michelangelo used the faces of his friends and acquaintances on the figures in his famous painting of *The Last Judgment*. And after he died, some of the figures were deemed too scantily dressed and clothing was painted on them!

Painter Daniele da Volterra was assigned to do the job, and it earned him the nickname "Braghettone," which means "pants maker."

One of the most famous details in this painting is the *Creation of Adam*, which shows God holding out his right hand to Adam. In the center of the painting, their fingers are very close together, but not touching. This is supposed to show that God can create something just by thinking about it. Their hands are very different: God's hand is strong and powerful, and Adam's hand is very relaxed, almost as if he'd just woken up.

THE TIBER ISLAND

Tiber Island is one of the most legendary places in the history of Rome. According to legend, after having driven out the last king, Tarquinius Superbus, the Roman people threw the grain from the king's fields into the river, forming a pile of debris that shaped the island.

But the roots of Tiber Island actually stretch much farther back — it was an important stop along the Tiber for migration between north and south. The island was also the center for worship of **Aesculapius**, the God of medicine, and a temple in his name was once located there. Now a church dedicated to **St. Bartholomew** stands on the spot. The island was also once used to quarantine the sick. The island has an unusual shape — it looks something like a boat — and is connected to the mainland by two bridges, **Ponte Cestio** and **Ponte Fabricio**.

THE PAPAL BASILICAS

The **Papal Basilicas** are the most important churches in the Christian world, with four large ones in Rome and two smaller ones in Assisi. They have special characteristics: a Holy door and a papal altar (St. Peter's in the Vatican also has the Holy See, the papal chair).

The Papal Basilicas in Rome are **St. Peter's** in the Vatican, which is the largest, **St. John Lateran**, the mother church of the diocese of Rome, **St. Paul's Outside the Walls** (image below) in the Ostiense district, and **St. Mary Major** on the Esquiline hill.

THE ROMAN ROADS

The Romans were skilled road builders: it's estimated that there were about 100,000 km of paved roads, and a further 150,000 km of dirt roads, thanks to which Roman civilization spread throughout the known world!

There's a famous proverb that says, **"All roads lead to Rome"**: the first and most important roads were built from Rome (in the forum there was the Golden Milestone, a small column that was used to measure distances) towards the main Italian cities and provinces in the empire, building bridges, tunnels and embankments as they went.

THE VIA APPIA ANTICA

The **Via Appia Antica** is called the "*regina viarum*" (the queen of roads) and was one of the most beautiful and important roads in ancient Rome. It was built by the consul Appius Claudius in 312 BC, and went from Rome to Campania. It was flanked by miles of tombs belonging to the most important Roman noble families, and today it is one of the most beautiful and evocative roads in the city, passing through the **Ancient Appian Park**.

On this road, there is the **Tomb of the Scipios**, the **Tomb of Priscilla**, the huge **Villa of Maxentius**, the famous **Tomb of Cecilia Metella**, and the majestic **Villa of the Quintili**, which was later turned into a medieval fortress.

THE CATACOMBS

Underneath Rome, there is a large network of dark and mysterious tunnels: the catacombs! This is where the first Christians buried their dead in antiquity.

The walls of these tunnels were filled with tombs which could contain more than one body. They were painted with very beautiful frescoes, illuminated by the flickering light of torches. Two of the largest and most famous are the **Catacombs of Saint Sebastian** and the **Catacombs of Saint Callixtus**, which overlook the Via Appia Antica.

ROME FOR KIDS

Useful contacts

N.B. Many of the activities are at weekends.
Please consult the reference site.

⭐ **Bioparco**, www.bioparco.it - Villa Borghese, Viale del Giardino Zoologico, 20

⭐ **Casina di Raffaello**, www.casinadiraffaello.it - Villa Borghese, Viale Casina di Raffaello, 19

⭐ **Cinecittà World**, www.cinecittaworld.it - Via Irina Alberti

⭐ **Cinema dei Piccoli**, www.cinamadeipiccoli.it - Villa Borghese, Largo M. Mastroianni, 15

⭐ **Explora**, www.mdbr.it - Via Flaminia, 82

⭐ **Leonardo da Vinci Experience**, www.leonardodavincimuseo.com - Via della Conciliazione, 19

⭐ **Luneur Park**, www.luneurpark.it - Via delle Tre Fontane, 100

⭐ **Museo delle Civiltà**, www.museocivilta.cultura.gov.it - Piazza Guglielmo Marconi, 14

⭐ **Orto Botanico**, www.ortobotanicoitalia.it - Largo Cristina di Svezia, 23a

⭐ **Parco regionale dell'Appia Antica**, www.parcoappiantica.it - Via Appia Antica, 42

⭐ **Planetario e Museo Astronomico**, www.planetarioroma.it - Piazza Giovanni Agnelli, 10

⭐ **Technotown**, www.technotown.it - Via Lazzaro Spallanzani, 1

⭐ **Welcome to Rome**, www.welcometo-rome.it - Corso Vittorio Emanuele II, 203

© 2021 Sassi Editore S.r.l. "Conosci ed Esplora Roma"
Viale Roma, 122b - 36015 Schio (VI).
© 2022 ARCHEOLIBRI S.r.l.
Via Romeo Rodriguez Pereira 102A - 00136 Roma
Tel. 02 94.75.99.70 - 06 354.970.514
www.archeolibri.com - info@archeolibri.com
Gruppo Lozzi Editori - www.gruppolozzi.it
"Guide of Rome Kids" ISBN 9788866680888

Illustrations: Matteo Gaule, Nadia Fabris, Dario Calì.
Graphics: Sassi Editore S.r.l., Fabiana Benetti, Francesco
Trupputi, Lozzi Graphics.
Texts by: Fabiana Benetti, Ester Tomè.
Traslations: TperTradurre S.r.l.
Printed by: C.S.C. Grafica S.r.l. - Guidonia (Rm)